BOUNDLESS
FUNCTION

LE MORTE D'ARTHUR
£250 ESSAY PRIZE

JUDGE: FRANK KERMODE

Poets, philosophers, readers and students of literature, unravel the secrets of *Boundless Function*, and you could win £250.

Le Morte D'Arthur Prize will be awarded for the best creative essay or critical review submitted to the publishers. The treatment may be general or particular to one aspect of the book. Articles already published in journals (or under consideration) may be submitted for the Prize as long as this is stated in a covering note.

There is no restriction on length, so that any article about *Boundless Function* is eligible – from a newspaper review to an extended exegesis.

Articles should be submitted by 31 December 1988, either as typescripts or as photocopies in the case of published essays. The judge's decision will be final, and no correspondence will be entered into with entrants regarding the judging at any stage.

Address for submissions: Le Morte D'Arthur Prize, Bloodaxe Books Ltd, P.O. Box 1SN, Newcastle upon Tyne NE99 1SN.

BOUNDLESS
FUNCTION

ARTHUR GIBSON

Edited by
A. ROYALE

With an Epigraph by
Academician G. Nedsmar
Institute for Cosmic Research
Melasurej

BLOODAXE BOOKS

ISBN: 1 85224 038 5

First published 1987 by
Bloodaxe Books Ltd,
P.O. Box 1SN,
Newcastle upon Tyne NE99 1SN.

Bloodaxe Books Ltd acknowledges
the financial assistance of Northern Arts.

Typesetting by Bryan Williamson, Manchester.

Printed in Great Britain by
Bell & Bain Limited, Glasgow, Scotland.

Is it indeterminate that Frank Kermode's room is on this picture? True or False? (Clue: it is not in the Chapel.)

To Frank Kermode

in appreciation and thanks

'But let your communication be, Yea, yea;
Nay, nay: for whatsoever is in excess of
these cometh of evil.'

MATTHEW 3:37

An early picture of the author when he was subconsciously composing the present work.

Editorial Preface

I thank Professor Frank Kermode for suggesting that I produce an edition of Arthur Gibson's unpublished manuscript *Boundless Function*, together with his advising me on the decision to include footnotes, as well as his drawing to my attention the possible existence of relevant material by Academician G. Nedsmar. The result of the latter is the Epigraph; this is a fragment of a larger work whose contents Gibson came upon as the stimulus for *Boundless Function*. Another factor which should be positioned is that of Gibson's membership of Professor Kermode's research seminar on the interpretation of narrative at King's in 1982, at the time *Boundless Function* was composed, although none of the material was either presented or discussed there. And the author has requested that a note of appreciation about this and other contact with Professor Kermode be expressed.

In some form, all the footnotes are from the hand of Gibson. It is clear that these are an integral part of the composition, although in the typescript they occupy various positions as marginal, textual or footnote expansions of the narrative.

Something of a mystery surrounds Gibson's leaving the manuscript in the present layout, although it is clearly in its final intended form. Professor Kermode tells me that this is precisely part of its creative merit, at one level being a new, *a genre* class; and in the light of other impending publications, this final form will be seen to be part of an overall cluster of innovations which mutually inform one another, though this is not to invite divination.

I am extremely grateful to Professor Kermode for his enlightening my editorial load by his having three times read and checked through the typescript during composition and in its present form.

A. ROYALE
Bacup, July 1987

9

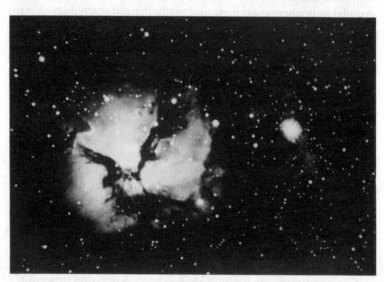

This Trifid Nebula in Sagittarius has attracted science fiction writers. But the truth about the Universe may be so stranger than fiction that a rational animal might be too indoctrinated to want to recognise it.

Epigraph[1]

Logic is much more unexpected than Frege thought. Frege was mistaken to regard tone as neither true nor false. His view of tone is not entailed by his logic. Tone is a logical element in a consistent creative language. 'Tone' is a term for the set of higher levels in an expression operating above and upon the primary sense. Thus tone's object-languages are the lower levels in an expression. This has its parallel in mathematical logic and mathematical cosmology. Meaning is not linear. It is multi-dimensional. Its topology is akin to General Relativity, but not to Euclid. Tone corresponds to the fourth dimension. Small differences are cosmic. Different cosmologies split off from each other over infinitesimal variations. Yet the resulting universes are fundamentally opposed. So it is with tone.

The cosmologies theoretically possible for General Relativity are said to be infinite. Thom's catastrophe mathematics may map the discontinuities. In his theory, whole systems are decomposable into other ones. The vector field of this discontinuity corresponds to the shift in consciousness for the logic of a genius's creative writing. In creation-cosmology physical constants 'go infinite' (for example the speed of light) in the Quantum Era of creation and before time zero. The deep structure of this topology would match the perfect creative use of language. Such creativity runs away with finite universals and creates new ones of infinite value. Genius ceases to be timebound. The sense of the universe is born from the void.

Creative possibility lies outside mechanical decision procedures. General Relativity was discovered by creative insight; but it is still logical. Even General Relativity collapses in the Quantum Era. Supergravity takes over: infinity overrides the establishment cosmology to create a new one. This is parallel with inspired poetry: cosmology of semantic miracle.

Just as the first few microseconds of spacetime condense from infinity so that the universe's various local physical systems are produced in the microseconds, similarly poetry disposes the sense of other genres: universalised discourse is the poetry of logic. Not all poetry satisfies this pattern. Yet that poetry which does is the set of all genres manifested as theorems of other genres. In this way true poetry is both logic and autobiography engaged to express universal-

---

[1] Taken from Дорӧджык пуктан, пыдысьджык босьтан , 1982, pp. 7-8.

ity. Autobiography, because cosmology is the autobiography of the universe, and autobiography of a person is his cosmology.

Consequently, the logic of this poetry would be both cosmology and personal autobiography. The ideal is a perfect fit between cosmology and autobiography. This contradicts the notion of *genres* as a criterion for distinguishing types of creativity. Such poetry as fits the above specification is *a genre*, as Professor Kermode has noticed.

Such poetry is *a genre* because it is the set of all sets of which it is not a member. At one level this would correspond to Hugh Everet III's universal wave function for the Universe as a quantum object with causality restored. This would show that Stephen Hawking's[2] view is incorrect when he proposed that there 'might be angels who could observe the Universe from outside but they could never communicate the results of their observations to us because, if they could, they would be part of the Universe and would be governed by the same laws, including quantum mechanics, as the rest of the Universe.' Physical laws do not stipulate necessity, but only contingency. Genius (while avoiding the Romantic and Classical associations of

The deep structure of the Universe is parallel with human experience. Jupiter's moon Io illustrates this. The Voyager 1 rocket series identified a volcano erupting on Io (as above). Catastrophe mathematics has been used to measure everything from volcanoes to births on earth. It is an underlying principle of life. Catastrophe precedes birth.

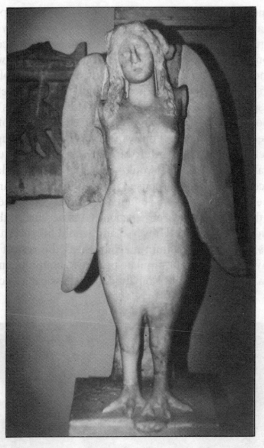

A genre is supposed to be one sort of type. But Classical culture constantly violated this recipe by joining unrelated, or keeping apart connected, things. Consider the ancient prechristian Greek statue above. It has properties: angel's wings (from which Christianity won its angels); the breasts, hair and hint of pregnancy suggest womanhood; the bestial feet and thighs advertise a goat-man. The latter is a satire, a Canaanite term for "goat-devil" which was imported to Corinth (1 Corinthians 10 alludes to this ancestry, stating: 'I would not that ye should have fellowship with devils', which is a quotation from Deuteronomy 32:17 where the original setting of Canaanite devil-worship's use of satire is being attacked). From one standpoint, therefore, this statue is an obscenity, although from another it coherently integrates an ancient perception of the sublime. But it is clear that the statue could not dance on the point of a pin. The true answer to the old question is that an infinite number of angels can dance creatively on a pin.

13

this term) has a physical analogue beyond General Relativity; from beyond this point angels would speak. This has its parallel in mental creativity. Culture is fiction when performed below the boundaries of material cosmology. Truth is culture when genius transcends the limits of its time in space-time: the metrics for true creativity are discontinuous with respect to its causal antecedents though derived from them. A human being is not merely the sum of its physical properties: 'Know ye not, ye are gods'. Turing's "oracle machine" can be programmed by the ideal realist artistic observer. The resulting creativity will reflect a group of theorems manifesting cosmology and autobiography. The oracle would decide the semantics. In this way, autobiography can be allegorical. God is the solution to Russell's Paradox. This remark is logical, astrophysical, and literary. The acceptance of genres as criteria, and university departments as distinctions about subject-borders, prevents apprehension of this remark, for those who labour under its stress.

ACADEMICIAN G. NEDSMAR
translated by A. Royale

---

[2] S.W. Hawking, 'Quantum Cosmology': Lectures given at the Leshouches Summer School, France, July 1983, p.3.

BOUNDLESS
FUNCTION

ARTHUR GIBSON

Translated from the original by the author

Three live metaphors, one personifying meaning.

16

The end of punctuation exhaled
Death's final breath
And the genres decayed to dust in the new beginning.

Ending is a form of death's birth in typical reverse.
There is an apocalyptical[1] story that I journeyed
far from home, and after a long time I chanced[2]
down the street which led on to Manningham Lane,
along which I passed Lord Lister[3] – swinging at
him my nappy in the air which had been somewhat
subject to Brownian[4] motion, it not occurring
to me at the time that metaphorical discourse is
live at times of lawlike movements of sense, with
a double reference as with a false stage in two
spectacles to taunt on meaning. This fine optician
with offices on Manningham was – later on – to give
me my first Hebrew beginning, he went to the head
of things, a true lord who was no dead metaphor
like Lister. Eventually mum found me, yet again,
to my now not incontinent joy, with her mock myopia
scatological on the sight which gladdened her eyes
before the approach of himself, encouraging me to
face the similitude apparently[5] of the Lord without
leprous intention to void the sentences which
riddled my zestful ease in her arms of seed's
fortune, a joyful happiness, just like Bradford's[6]
grandfather (a surrogate father, the first of a
regal line) sat me on his knee to read his past's
future for me, a blessed haven of Jacob's
encampment[7] stilled against the stir of paralysed
memory's home unaware as I was of domestic ease's
absence from my home, while I yet yearning for the
the stable[8] tack's unknown support, not knowing,
but registering the hardly suppressed nervous
fidget of ageing fingers' recoil on the chair's
arm at my whispered innocence an unconscious
mirror[9] of paternal rages of the screaming pope[10]
who threw his child across the room to dash its
head against the square of wood.

Is it right to write all thoughts as sentences? The New Testament's early manuscripts have no punctuation. Was this intentional? May some thoughts have a non-sentence structure? Why not let the mind use its own thought-structure as a pattern for punctuation? The author photographs meaning, and the picture is no sentence. Why not turn abstract thought into word pictures? Punctuation is thus partly removed from print, while the thought, like a radio telescope, interprets undivided impressions of a universe.

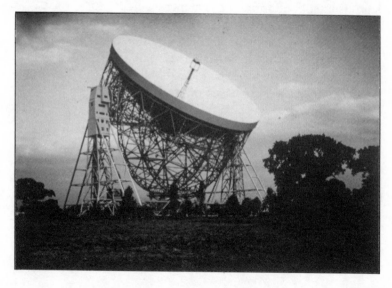

Grandfather died as suddenly as this. Knowing
from him that I would nevertheless see him again
I wept for myself, not knowing what balance was
found wanting with part of me gone and alone
except for mum and the stranger in my midst, yet
unborn with hope's seed.

The function:[11]

In beginning was the word
And the word was God's presence
And God was the word
This was: In beginning, the God's presence
All through it[12] came to be
And without it nothing came to be
that which has come to be
in it was life
And the light was the life of the men
And the light shines in the darkness
But the darkness did not grasp it.

'The Oracle' was the title of the Holy of Holies in Solomon's Temple (and is the source of 'The Word' – 'The Logos' of John's Gospel). It had to compete with many female mother gods such as Hathor, the cow goddess. Her atmospheric temple at Denderah, though, serves as an indirect influence on Christian cathedral architecture, whilst 'The Oracle' is ground plan for the mind.

Given a set of premises (such as corporation[13]
houses, one in which I lived since five to
nineteen), and two propositions – any you
like to entertain – you assert another proposition
– any you like to entertain. And that follows
my leader; but the leader smiles and does not
know why it follows. The problem is about why
the rule cuts. One has to consult The Oracle.[14]
The Oracle is the overtone of the Logos, and
that's logic. I now occupy the third proposition,
knowing hardly how I got there, there is more
to it than instinct, even though God is tricky.
Once becoming, or should I say holding to a
value of the proposition, the third proposition
can itself become a premise for habitual usage.
In fact how long is a proposition? Senseless[15]
question. If the functions are consistent then
the values are infinite. This I sensed but could
not say when I lived in the corporation house,
sometimes appearing in a Macintosh[16] lashed by but
not to the clothes line in the hall of departure[17]
through the front door to search for other
premises without a penny in my mind but with
the sense of a beginning.

Meaning is a *proper* name[18] for someone like me who
was born under the Cow and Calf[19] Rocks of Ilkley
Moor which I do not remember although my present[20]
person is proof I was a pregnant product though
I cannot present the links which chain me to that
event despite its being inferred by my being
Meaning. (The fact that this inference can be made
shows that Jesus did not pre-exist, for who would
enter a second time into the womb?) Having made
my first appearance I was not one to retreat and
wait for a better time when there was no war-time
against spirit, although of course the first person
here is an anachronism because it was me then. Me
was a big enough problem lovingly developed from

The sacred boat by which the pharaoh went into the next world is a model for many an illusory journey in modern life.

mine hostess, without having sense or reference to
the first person; but had I thought, I might have
known the first person could not refer even then
because when I slept people used the name Meaning
to refer to me yet never with my first person nor
did I when I was sleeping, so you cannot substitute[21]
the first person for Meaning which refers. Perhaps
I is a predicate: a concept true of me but not
referring to me. This was the puzzle I had as a
child, I did not know I had a puzzle, and to which
bit of me did I attach with no reference to point to me?[22]

This was the first person. This was the
first person who never talked to me never to blemish
the silence of noise touched by the surface of
abducted substances like beer and urine. I still
fail to smell the difference of this silent stench
getting below language is impossible while you use
it; and it is not there to be above you when you
are under the sod's function without value. Still
since the past's person was left at a Dunkirk of
life after stowing away on a life's journey fleeing
the cancer of migration from poverty's Durham[24]
coalfield as with a morbid dread of confined faces
seeking the same life I am now discovering, we
ought not to suppose him to be sober enough to be
a shepherd's crook who failed although life's
contrary of this is not success for there are true
propositions, false statements, and valueless
propositions. But is truth boundless? And who
feels a proposition? The one who is the embodiment
of it. Can a proposition embody a feeling? If God
is love would it follow that he has to have a body?[25]
This body soon became overweight with this
blind intuition lubricated by the spirit of
insensibility's honesty.

Meaning's antecedent causes but does not condemn life. There were many levels in his language. His tragedy was a blow-out of a level in his meaning, not meaning itself; a whole philosophy of life cannot be tragedy consistently,[26] for how could you start without birth? Although he might have pursued a deformation of life's sensibility, who can generalise a physiology for grief's provocation unless it were watered by spirit masked and deflected by unacknowledged cessation of intercourse with the sympathetic familiar demons of tragedy, as he would presuppose his fellows to be, a genuine fear of invasion which was actually his evocation of sense, treading the recurrent rupture of male friendships made bearable by, but not seen by him to be in causal[27] conjunction with, the bed of casual body, insensibly seared by the ulcerated mind.[28]

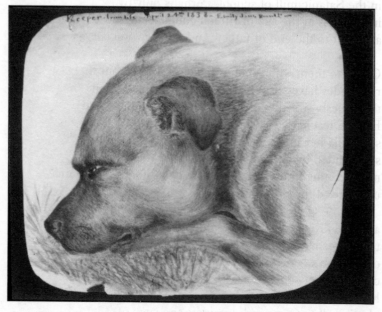

Once Emily Brontë was badly bitten by a dog; she took a blacksmith's red-hot iron and seared her arm. Her novel Wuthering Heights *is like this event. It sears culture in the pursuit of life.*

Of course it is impossible to do surgery
on the ulcer for when the mind is prodded through
the opened brain, the privacy of the mind is not
observable – gone to grass as I later did,
over Haworth's moors

                    (became industrial whores)[29]

went I for the joy of freedom's search in ignorance
of the ideal[30] observer's theory of meaning while
believing its theory of truth – though father no

longer retained it in his knowledge – but never
met Emily's beasts, only her wonder which has a
metaphysical prowess that is not easily blended
with the warp and woof of Bradford's bullswool.[31]

Not encompassing the quality, but feel the width
of the foursquare sheet mapping the fiction embodied
in the Satanic mill of school. Perhaps only two
in my class at the age of fifteen could recite the
alphabet to the end of father, and Hebrew was all

Greek to them with no knowledge of Greek, but the
remainder have since learned various sentences at
the majesty's displeasure. I only now remember the
English teacher's brave pleasure, a face of
sensibilia her impression left within me somewhere,
surrounded by Cretan riot a Santorini volcano, with
me excreting in my pants out of fear of home's ignorance
unaware of the present riot, then

                        jerkily stalking
as to be invisible across the foursquare yard to
the cleansing toilets, barely sensing the instinct
of hygiene's logic, blanked out by my emerging
chuckles, not sensed as grim, ascending to the
hysteria of bravado's seeming comedy gripped by the
plastic will to enjoy and dominate the suck of
Sam's company.

In about 1500 B.C. the Santorini volcano blew out the middle of the Aegean island of Thera, leaving a moon crescent shaped island with a large lagoon. Underneath the above ash the city of Akrotiri was unearthed; but it was found that much of the city had already been shaken by an earthquake at least a year before the eruption; this is known because remains of grass were found on top of house walls whose roofs had collapsed. It seems that the islanders left with their valuables and caused riot on Crete. Recent excavations show that Sir Arthur Evans was probably right in concluding that King Minos had united the Aegean by ridding it of island pirates (the thalassocracy *of Homer). This stable economic world started to break up, with the eruption on Thera; the non-Greek Minoan Linear A began its quick decline to a dead language, though its sign system was taken over and modified to write Greek in Linear B, and a major military defeat reduced Crete in about 1450 B.C. Thus the throne of King Minos (above) was vacated. It was only later in Rabbinic Hebrew that the term for 'throne' became a pseudonym for a toilet.*

The earth mother goddess of ancient Turkey is here guarded by leopard demigods. She was construed as the universal womb to which human sacrifice was offered. Originating in Sumer, she went with the leopards through Turkey into Greece, later to emerge as the feminised Dionysos with the leopards absorbed, championed by Euripides. In this way Classical tragedy is very ancient, just like the modern world experienced through Shakespeare.

The world imprisoning him in his heart[32]
a natural darkness grasping no light subjects
love to the plague of custom's rejects, an old
duke with spectacles eclipsing the sockets of
life civil void to cover the birth of a great
affliction I cast off for an encampment of
entreaty breathing the first air of the body
prepared for me kissing not the hand which smells
of the multitude in the valley of decision
enthralled with the additions of nothing will come
of an image on the coinage of infallibility's
knights in darkness. Within the void silence there
can be no aesthetics for silence opens no womb of
speech but takes away the heart of light. Standing
in the rain's torrent of abuse remembered wet with
immediate remembrance of hate's love a shrieking
wind to tear the face of childhood's sloppy stance,
one winter's evening returning to the tomb of home.
Did the unknown car stop with kind words of a mother's[33]
comfort to lift me in to receive the drying warmth
of words' concern? Yes, for the aim was not silence
but company a token of an absent child's attention
to his father's home, of sense's bolt by lane to
mother's home. Mum, not mother, really, in a noisy
solitude a peaceful tragedy of silent meaning alien
in the madness of fatherly adversity with bodies
one, hearts nil playing away all the time as the
winter of Christmas joy brings prospect's puppy,
exterminated for excreting on the carpet's figure
with conscientious objecting attracting the third
degree cigarette burns, to greet my return to house.

A brother in Christ in a water house introduced me
to the life, although I already knew the mason who
carved the metaphors, and his wife was Yahweh's
grace, yet like a quaker seed, made themselves my
new home in sensibility's novel discovery of
fretless beams enamoured me as an invisible college.[34]

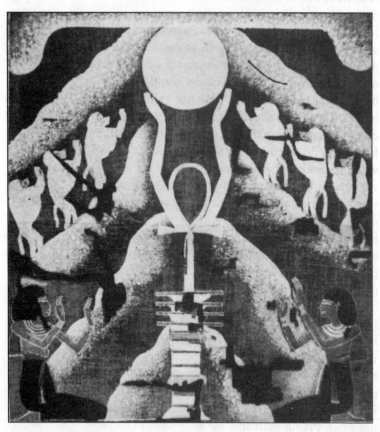

An Egyptian example of an attempt to make nature a map of what existence is. The loop-cross 'immortal soul' centrepiece praises the sungod with the help of evolving demigod baboons. Darwin seems to have been anticipated.

Writing did not then seem the most important thing.
Even if it were, this could not be so since it
could not sensibly preclude one from believing in
the given view of truth's importance, for living
is prior to writing it and truth is a necessary
condition of referring to it. But the direction
of reference is wrong: there is no route back[35]
from the thing to which I refer. Responding to
sense beyond our ken is not to know the route
though who can start from where they do not stand
or find themselves? The person I could not have
been might have said that 'I do not believe in
truth'. But this is already the disguised
contradictory which denies the intended sense.
If there is no truth how is the statement true
when nature's personification said 'All things
are relative' because all is here an impossible
word if nature were true. Nature's mind is no
map of ontology. And relative to what? The
incomplete expression mimics the endgame[36] of
determinate sensibility, which is a subjective
possible world of infinite variety tenanted by
the speaker rigidly designated but really fluid in a
congress of nature. But even this presupposes
truth in a possible world, at the expense of
truth's being primary; yet if we actually exist
we are not solely possibilities I am being referred
to by my name, not possibly referred. So truth is
primary and possibility secondary. And how could
I refer to a possible world where abstract objects do
not exist. Presumably one possible world can be
contrary to another world which is actual.[37] But how
would a child like me decide which to occupy? The
interpretation of narrative consists in more than
typology for the writer exists as does the world.
The child's identity though developing satisfies
a criterion signified by his proper name which on
occasions might be synonymous with the functions
of typology. Who is to say that patterns are

The Greek Athenian pantheon, as shown above in the Parthenon, is filled with a family of deities resembling humans. These fictions embody the imagination of those who depicted them. In Classical Greek, some of them were termed 'devils'; in Mark 3 Jesus is recorded as having identified the good Baalzebub as the Devil. Accordingly, these uses show ancient psychology which admits that humans are devils.

literary fictions? Even Hitler manifested father's
perception of Germany while yet a running left at
Dunkirk hiding like Obadiah's friend from the
soldiers of Baalzebub[38] along the coast of the
ships of Tarshish[39] unable to extract him from the wife's
kiss of contracting tuberculosis in the trenches
against the wall of manhood's fear to be invalided
out of the army and Baalzebub does not even refer
as a quasi-name for a focal point of Wagner's virtue;
but some people tumble behind the focus of political
idolatry's war-machinations of personal identity[40]
in the flux of freewill and providence's permission.
So who would blame a father's action after all this?
One can only hope that I am the antitypical format,
for are we not free to act in accordance with a
calculation.

The Devil is a false-god, not a god who is false,
the incarnation of human hearts' desire for a
possible world of fallacy. It is too convenient
that infinite possibilities slip their anchors or
reason; there is no theory of fallacy for
opposition to truth and confusion are not laws
of the Kingdom child's innocent enquiry, even
though distance from truth can be measured by the
meaning of narrative's coherence. A new child's
coherence is a delicate sensibility, but is not
arbitrary if he sat on the right knees (two children
might coherently be sitting upright on two people's
knees, but one would be upside down to the other,
if the children were far enough apart) so the
self-evidence of truth or coherence should not
be over-estimated without using the angel's
flax.[41] Even Jesus beheld Satan as lightning fallen
from heaven. Surface grammar is the emblem of
Baalzebub's agents; behind the world of fiction
the undertext comes from the world the undertext
of truth is the world. Surface grammar is Baal's
bible, the relativism of a possible world used

to mask the actual world, ambivalent over the
the will of the witch and the thing which is
will's target, the letter of the law manifested
as the spirit of the world: Hitler's blackened
formal splendour marched to the hymn of devotion's
anthems ancient and modernity clusters a modest
messiah a Kittel's word book[42] of betrayal at the
novice god's glister clyster ambient in god manifestation.
This, the latent sense of my early childhood, like
an idiom discontinuous with its internal senses,
thinking I would give my right hand to be
ambidextrous looking in the history's recent
mirror of the world alongside the figure in the
carpet, having no wish to kill the father, not
stronger in death dream, and discover an
infinite regress of the figure of the figure in the carpet
of the figure of the figure until Cantor's madness.

From the oblique mood my mother, ethnos, takes
it should not be thought that she is not the
mum. An embodiment of sensibility and guileless
peace, saddened by the passible rack of union's
trenchant blade but this did not thrust through
the gentle calm, suppressing but not seeming to
withhold the pressures of mad oppression from
without disarmed by an empathetic smile of helpful
strength amidward a visage of an ancient dignity
brought to be a presence of comfort for the
children a real aristocrat (without external
revolution though) as an aristocrat of regal
quality once said to me worthy of her motherhood
if that were possible in isolation without
altering other contexts nor imposing them (but
who can exist in a vacuum or choose his own; the
tares are not identifiable till after harvest –
we all look the same in the ark's coffin). As
mum could never have said, a proper name needs
a function to pick out its bearer (at least in
starting out to know someone), although once

Carved on the ceiling of the temple at Karnak is the cartouche of Rameses II. It is an encircled proper name. The proper name has not died, though its bearer has. So a bearer may be separated from his name, whilst his name cannot be severed from his identity. A temple of improper names is a box of fallacies.

done, the name of itself thereafter identifies
if the function is a criterion of identity. Names
are thus like life, part of language part of
life, dependent on dependant as a function of
realising identity but separated so that the
name is a universal although the context isn't.

But did she even become a function of herself
or a selfless function dominated by someone
else's name? This is the ambiguity, but no
weak duplicity enhances the ambivalent
apprehension for a singular epiphany was this
figure a solitary journey among near strangers
eyes as deep as wells which water not easily
but often disguised as with the summer's draught.
To preserve a great love where there is hate
and a madness of adversity when the objects of
love are terrorised into numb blind apprehension
unaware of personal relations needs strength of
a mystery to sustain life. This is why set in the
life's language is the sense of the divine life
even allowing for the differences of the persons
and not confusing the substance. The narrative
of tragedy and the ideal future are not metaphor
not analogy but the use of language as it is in
our usage, as my mum used to live in her oblivious
say. Her knowledge of God was personal and not
metaphorical believing as she did in the birth
which Christ's revelation gave to literal
description of God to which the moor's atheist
fiddling in Luddendenfoot (not in the region
of Cleckheckmindsedge) might have said: eyeballs
God has not, to which I respond (being the likeness
of herself) those perceptually rotting orbs you
term eyes, like an eyeless duke, curtailed in
the human form, are not the ideal eye with which
to see that God has eyes, but merely marbles
which you have lost to Mr Glass, damn
them. Even with the glass eye you might see beyond
the false knows that colour is used of different
colours, but it is not analogical or metaphorical:
God knows he is good is love is wise I knows it is
in any case within the discourse that words come
to be known, measured matched contrasted distanced
related under literal sense's dominion is a
parable of the heavens declare[43] the glory of God

36

in the appropriate semantic rule here a cosmos
there a line's proverb which darkness cannot grasp
in grope's[44] day, but our old house was invisible
seen above this silvery vapour in whichever
place the soul lives to give sense to the
narrative not solely figura. But mum embodied
this without I think conscious formulation as
with two widely different uses of the one term
with a relation between both quite proper but
perhaps with one unaware of the other to be supposed to
anthropomorphise language may therefore may after
all universals be to bring out the sense of the
ideal word without of course alluding to a
bewitched form of Plato's heaven, but with Emily's
Donne, yet not imprisoned as earth in Charlotte's

Christianity's 'immortal soul' came from Plato's Phaedo *which he wrote in his Academy outside Athen's centre, only just now being excavated and dried out under cover. Greek philosophy absorbed the teaching from Babylonian, and in turn Babylon derived it from the Sumerian ZU. So is the Christian soul Sumerian?*

literary birth.[45] So it is important not to
define a word by reference to only one type
of object of which it is true, nor by objects.
Referring is a piece of meaning, but reference
is not. Stay within the game of life's sense,
but this is not to remove reference from the sense
to point the way of ontology for speech is
part of how we are to be; but to look at mum
you had to see within to know the sense beyond
the world of face's grammar lined with the
theorems of the mind's eye, evident only to the
insider's poem the difference between suffering
and tragedy.

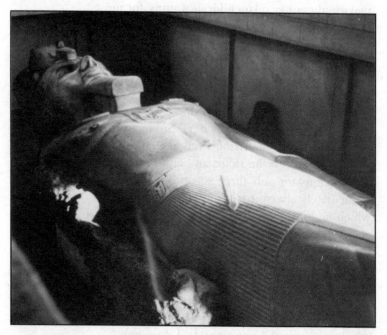

*Some of the large statues of pharaohs derive from the assumption that they
were incarnations of giant gods. This notion seems to have emerged from
Babylon, perhaps taken to Egypt by early invading Sumerians. A main
Canaanite word for 'giant' means 'healer' (rapha', plural rephaïm), and
a mortuary temple has been found dedicated to the Rephaim. This term
is the source for the 'Shades' and they were believed to inhabit the under-
world. Their personal identity was consequently unclear, and they died out.*

She would never say curse God and die gone from
mind's eye, although cry in an understanding
voice walking mind's hill, places and paths
through gate and door, simple but excellent
in understanding things, speaks the truth nothing
perverse no gold or silver nor rubies; leaving
substance as sole inheritance, a sort of
metaphoric existence (not that existence is
a metaphor, the metonymy is live not dead): a
form of the amen bringing up the children;[46]
one might say, alternatively, I was established
as the I will be, her delights being pure with
the sons of men where the habitat was possible
making them her own children waiting for me
at door at gate, although if the pronoun of the
first person does not refer then this use of
the 'not quite equivalent of he himself' is a
stencil for me and not exclusively I so to
speak.

 It was at this time that the door was
slammed in my face (not by her). Subject to
a given form of concussion I fell like an
unhealed giant to the floor, and although
unconscious for only three seconds, I[47]
immediately afterwards said: who am I, to
which he himself responded: Meaning has had an
accident, to which I sympathetically said: He
has had one as well, has he, not realising Meaning
was I. I did not appreciate at the time that
this, among other things, showed that I did
not necessarily refer, or to put the point
more strongly (although this raises the issue
of whether it is the same point), I does not
refer, since identity is in question. Sadly
at this time of age of twelve, being somewhat
paralysed in person, I did not know my identity
not in the sense of I am Meaning with respect
to such and such a property (since we lived
in a rented corporation house), but that this
was not a mental event which ever occurred to

me, recognising myself in the mirror though
I did this is not quite the same (with respect
to the property) as having a conception of
the identity that one is, and how large is
the proposition which houses the property of
identity: enough to recognise the body.
Well no confusion about that especially when
you are treated like a body, but how could
even a body want to be a body, without mind
going ontological in the form of a proposition
of identity.

      I was only once propositioned
by a sodomite,[48] as a child, at a bus stop, late
at night, a man of age and stench of moral
pustules upon his leering face I ran as
terrified from San Francisco now knowing that
my identity did not belong in that world of
impending earthquake,[49] so also coming to sense
that exclusion of possibilities contributes
towards the formulation of conceiving of
one's identity, although even this conflates
derivative possible futures with present
identity. But do not try to reduce me to
a location in space time, I am no engaging
here or *this* with which to demonstrate as
with a gesture the door to the property. I
believe. What I believe is the thought; the
thought is the object of my believing. *This*,
this is not a this. So the proposition of
identity is the thought. The thought of I
is not the same truth as I; the former is
indirect. But I had no conception of this
when fleeing with instinct the thought of
his identity a masque on his face whose latent
presence was envisaged as faecal countenance of
void. If thought were invested with sense
by use of words, so that face would decompose
into harromog before a mirror. Happily I had
no aim to look in the mirror!

40

Creeping into the bed of private chthonic death

of sleeping exploration hiding from the blade
of day's custom,
                    as I work to dream the real mice
run over my sheets and terrify the child of
hope to escape the droppings are there again

in the morning's cold torture a lear of drabness
cannot shovel them up for the oblivion of the
formal possibilities of fiction cannot reduce
this memory to the dung of historical novelty
in which the literary man may submerge my past.

It refers, though the pattern has no reference
to my memory of the lizard I brought home but it
soon vanished in that bedroom. Did the mice eat
or did it escape the pattern? Perhaps they were
rats
      but imagination has its limits even then
when I thought within the restrictions of sane

fear it was not a possibility with which to
engage sensible fright like the radio which teased

out my nerve because of its systematic fiction
a science apart from me as the house's only
entertainment as I thought. Imagined possibility

by me are under the control of whatever I am, but
external possibilities run the metaphor
                                        out of
control[50] down the slope and perish a legion of
dishonour are we they might have said.

Kept under raps.[51]

The bowls of judgement poured out over the earth in The Revelation cause the Euphrates to dry up. As a result of this the dragon (probably Sebeok-Tannin, a little known Egyptian crocodile god-hybrid) has frogs crawling out of his mouth. The frog-demons were imagined occupants of Sumerian swamps near the Persian Gulf, and such ideas were imported into Ethiopia, rather like the frog god from the Island of Meroe. These early images are used figuratively in The Revelation to signify political powers possessed by them, which were conceived to dry up Mesopotamian wealth, and then the demons were to invade Europe via Turkey (Anatole). Thus the King's gate in ancient Turkey at Hattusha is where the Hittites placed a god to block the demons' way to the West. It seems clear that this did not stop them.

But in the dark
                    where a butter shaw does not flow one
can see that the heavens declare a calculation
out of God's glory to assure any fear of desolation

where the sun makes its journey to lighten a bare
ontology or a freak
                    of poverty's exploration to
enrich even a child unknowing of such consequent
sonship dominated by a future unknown
                                        Lord true
and righteous are thy judgements the sun heat
blasphemed the name of God was full
                                    of darkness
darkness gnawed the pain the great river Euphrates

and the water dried up Anatole unclean[52] spirits
frogs came out of the dragon gather to battle the
battle day mageddon voice out of the temple.

I awoke in the dark to day sure the frogs were not
the mice
            (it is not a possibility that they were
the narrative does not offer infinite opportunities[53]
for variable ascription)
                        so I had not to make a
self-conscious move to cope with the as yet dead
awareness of the context
                        of my self, but
protected from the carnal outsider seeing from
without the parable of life grope grasp in the
dark apprehension of the keys which open and

shut the universe of discourse: loose the womb
of the bound opportunity to enter the tomb
from which to go no more out in a consecration
of I will be who I will be as one brought up
to be a pillar of sorts leaving the pillow for
for good.

This altar came from a Classical Greek temple. Probably in the 8th century A.D. it was placed in a Byzantine church whose present form is pictured above, in the Agora of Athens, a few yards from where Socrates died. Typically, there is nothing new under the sun. How Greek Orthodox are the Classics?

A relation of the water house sat before me a
child I sat with the others around[54] they being
men of the world's eclectic few and he being
in the role of the man of the world I not seeing
his relation to this other world around me nor
blithe in my ignorance of the eclectic eclipse
of it as he the older one sat before me giving
an image of the role of man of the world said
anything is possible with the others scant
askance in their position of impossibility.
There was no context principle for me to use
of this man's words other than my own desire to
rid myself of the impossible restrictions of
birth only in the context of a function does
such an opportunity have no meaning if you want or
are going to cancel me I might have thought, but
at eleven I sat as he sat and was no longer
astonied at my, my hope: an unintended value
takes to the function. This often happened my
world in temporary conjunction with a passing
star (as he thought himself possibly to be) which
though Wormwood a golden altar to me with no
relativity in the *to me* but a realist theory of
meaning utilising a universal function, as I came
to recognise it, a burning lamp fell from heaven;
but this is no catastrophe only if you mark it as
no living creature would appear to be in the
fountains of waters. He was really there tracking
some Saul or alternatively Obadiah (although this
did Ahab no good waiting in his dry desert, for
when the waters come they are bitter).

But I was not
smitten even though sun moon stars darkened
day for the inhabiters O earth. So I climbed out
of the pit of Sunday's school after this counsel
of possibility in which the messengers of God had
carefully helped me beyond the billiard tables
and bar there arose the smoke of men's pleasures,
as Stanley the wise fowler had taught me. A
blessed man who wept at division of the spirit's
labour (although I knew not this at the time)
and instructed me in the art of history's
possibilities and necessity concerning the locusts,
a scorpion, suffering a negation of the proverb

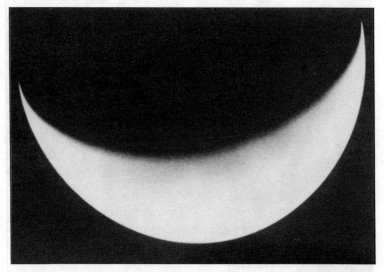

*We might fail to recognise an example of something we know: the above
sunrise on Venus may be misperceived as an earthly moon or eclipse of the
sun, and not as a goddess of love.*

with a king over them. Esther like me knew that
there is no destruction by these for those who
hold to the horns of the altar and pray when
surrounded by Mahamet, as Stanley might have said
when stumbling to the funeral of the mason, for it
is a short wait for the man with feet as pillars of fire in
temple's entrance if the architecture is not
romantic octavo where they worship devils whom
even Manningham's optician could not treat in
the strip of gold silver brass stone wood for
the feast is under way.

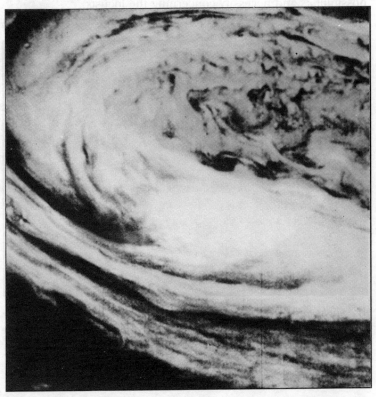

*Likewise clouds racing across a sky might not be recognised for what they
are: the shifting Great Red Spot on Venus.*

People were less blind in Jesus' day, but still blind: they recognised the weather, but not the signs of the times, though clouds above over the Greek island of Ithaca are not seen by Odysseus now.

World lines run parallel but the lives are
discontinuous as I found a marvellous cloud of
sense drifting over the sun's value shot
                                    with
lightning's vibrant photograph in the mind's
incense as the clouds raced across
                            heaven
from a far country in haste
                        to meet the rush
of the dayspring of Mordecai's return. This
helps the bellyache,
                    as does the honey.

Had I thought, leaving school at fifteen
was freedom but not for the usual redress
the vocational labour working before school
after school all weekend all holidays in
gross shop from the age of eleven onwards near
covert by the excursion into imagination, dullness[55]
extended by the late hours of opening's insults
those familiar cheap expensive late night whimsy
shops of slum corporation estate in which to become
no legal person ought to live though without mumble
a grumble at the past discontent since to be
the people there deserve the status and distant
position of the overlords who have deprived[56]

*The remains of the ancient town slum for the workmen (of Deir el medina)
who worked on the Royal Tombs in the Valley of Kings, whose living
conditions were bad enough to match those of some modern inner cities.*

them of them masked by filth, lice, bugs, rats
decay, disease of the soul sometimes attended
by the medical man whose only crutch was a lunch
booze no Boaz for the womb of hope, though patients
in cheerless mask together to steer away the dredge
of policed officiated problems inside with the
mock of aid social service and unemployed pain
to eat away the heart of stomach's acids in a
drab rust for political priority and agonies,
many unsaid and strange, not extrinsic to personal
identity nor only a visage[57] of will but matter
is not everything there is no way will has to
go in the heart of the age's pattern's disposition.

Is there a parallel between the social services of ancient Egypt and modern society? The lordly Amenhotep of Kom Ombo receives medical attention with prescriptions and medical instruments, but he did not risk catching Aids in hospital.

Ancient Philistine housing was often better than some modern U.K. corporation housing, this restored house at Tel Qasile illustrates (in the Philistine Gaza Strip excavations). Unlike some modern democratic government policy, at least the Philistines specified and confidently recognised what were to be their human sacrifices.

As being the child which had not occurred to
what it was to be I am, from which it eventually
followed (but not immediately, which would an
illogical, how like a, theologian would reason)
that I knew not where I stood to see the beauty
of holiness quit like a Philistine. However in

the morning all the eastern masses of enemies
were dead[58] as I came to the valley with a beck
where I played the witting savage red[59] turned
the stream within my eyes. Still I saw boundaries
to objects but not to time, unless down stream
there was an iceberg son who melted away in
a flux of confusion. But I might have realised
that a proposition about time does not have to
be as long or short or sliced just because or
if time came to be; that would be the sort of
category-error even then I had instinctive sense
to avoid the collapse of sense and reference, for
playing down the beck[60] I saw that even in Bradford
I was locked in the present but not space to
breath since place is not tensed, even if angels[61]
dance on a pinhead (not a French one) which is
rather a silly theology, but which theologian
worries now?, one does not share here but why not
share now unless you are some sort of solipsist?
But even then you have the possibility of sharing
now, but not then try making time a causal
relation yet I could not then grasp the sense
of darkness but had causal relations with
objects as I looked down space to the valley's
end, but who could have looked down its time
that would take time but my look down the valley
was timeless. The stream where we played
disappeared into a tunnel obscured by the
surface culture from the mill; too risqué,
so home to Zeno's but not through it. Mind you
my language might have been too weak to define
the relevant notions in it;[62] although that did
not seem obvious to me at the time nor even now
because I never was a politician or theologian –
as the boldness and the thinness of the claim
thereof, although they might try to get around
the weakness of their sentences by adding a
set or two but even then they would end up in
the usual paradoxes of labour's choice because

The temple to the sea god Poseidon stand at the end of Greece facing East towards Delos where Poseidon's 12 brother gods journeyed from Greece via water.

the delphic oracle does not stop the water running
into the tunnel even though I had dammed the water
many times in a race against the drift of words.
But one question remained: if I filled a number
of cans with water I could infer at least one
can of water from them; now could I infer a
number of cans of water from just one can of
water (or one just can, does the difference
matter)?

The problem is to distinguish between a foundation
and a starting point of the man child; the same
is true of the world's knowledge, but I did not
know this when confusing point with foundation
in fact not knowing what the point of starting
was nor the foundation's meaning but I was no
Constantine, a converse Joseph, speak to so,
with stars, dragon, woman and all spewed out
over the Latin wilderness like some neoplatonist
acting out Protagoras for a tautology of three
and a half days of no rain with stars falling around.

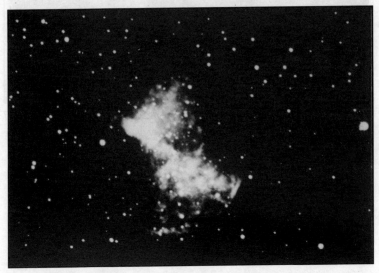

Like the Roman Empire, a galaxy explodes and stars fall to the night ground.

The author's future life in Athens, finding that it is much like all other cities.

Well, I thought, sitting there in
Bradford going for a burton's[63] satanic career,
with all this confusion, and intense albeit dim
dam vision, what is the difference: Bradford or
Ilkley is it to be? Anyway is there any seeded
difference between Ilkley and Jerusalem, Bradford
and Athens? But what about Rome's role in revising
ontology and the future's haven? The wool and
silver lining manufacturers I discovered could not
tell the difference between I am and I will be.
But this was not the case in Heckmondwyke in the[64]
vale of the shadow of Cleckheckmindsedge, visiting
there in earnest wing looking for a form of truth
without denying the power of roots uninterested
in the material vermin and discovering that a
starting point is not an establishment,
although the establishment's strappings
trappings nearly possibly might have hooded
the yen lest said soonest ended, Shebna-like
without the key to the heavens openers shutters
loosers binders manufacturing had not then
started to decline so the Pullman train of
commerce was not transparent yet. I like
riding on steam, but not that one. I hardly
realised at the time of dawning self-consciousness
if 'some child' were to refer although it cannot
I would then have said the thought refers in
different ways: a childhood with different
seeming extensions of actually possibly possibly
possibly (this could go on modal worlds to come[65]
but not to be) identities of the imagination's
youth's man child; but denotes does not refer –
just as the Keynes' economy[66] refers to no reality
(i.e. does not refer) like: *blank* has some
indeterminate relation to *blank*. I was never a
blank pretending to refer, but at least always
filled with possible content while discerning
the abstract reality but not abusing the reference.

A photograph was taken about this time upon
Ilkley Moor above the Cow a long way from Shipley's
fairies but not the plural of twelve the wisdom
of which already guided me without my sensing it.
I do not remember this (I find I can remember
nothing before the age of fifteen, with mind
ironed with a devil's sear, or perhaps it was a
just my response to cool and more than exist
in such affairs of nullity) and only recognised
myself in it when it was drawn to my memory
(it is odd how memory covers as a law what is
true and what is false without distinguishing
the role of the imagination and the attention
of its introspection) and there I stood (with
now no mere denotation but is not a photograph

a sentence) against the eyeballs (a secular
phanerosis photographing likeness on the brain-
flesh of the senses, I thought I might have, it
soon occurred to me in Heckmondwyke when later
thinking about this image when reading John –
at one level add Thomas – now here's a proper
name referring not denoting) but I did not see
my self in the photograph only the trappings
of flesh and company without angels (which is
not to say they were not there) nor realising
that the self is not invisible but me under

the appropriate criterion: I might have said
what is behind my self in the photograph? The
proper reply: Ilkley Moor, would have eluded
the balls of mind.

*On the Greek Island of Delos there is a range of mountainous temples to
the gods of Canaan who have migrated there, attracted by Greek interest.
But the main Greek god Dionysos still had his sanctuary, and at the front
corners were raised statues of his symbol, pictured above but broken off —
as is the fate of such gods.*

The eel is caught in the author's past.

Another photograph of an earlier stage in my
self was a trip with what might have been a
dale from the moors, fresh fine (but owing to
this strange state my mind was in I did not
know what it was to have friends although I
had friends, and this does not now seem to be
that childlike oblivion of relations to enjoy
which is normal whatever it would be to be
normal) to Scarborough we were taken and caught
an eel. But it was only the photograph which
was my memory of the time; I looked happy,
even though I could not swim (these waters I
still fear to tread). Mine host informs me in
later years that a vigour of mischief was my
patter of tiny foibles irksome in its extremity
occasionally to some of those around populated
as I was with future's distorted possibilities,
even though having a peer of sentiment's Nazi
tending Branwell but pushed aside as tardy after
the usual comic adsorption. Imagine if imagination

60

corresponded to expressions on my face, and a
criterion of recognition were that of identity,
perhaps this is how I acted as if (but without
conceiving it) I would have envisaged myself to
be; but this criterion even then would be a
necessary and not sufficient condition for my
we I can see me to be.

How to heal the water's mirror of me then,
not like treading out corn, and pour the cruse
to desterilise the barren influence. Forty-two
other children (a small typical class for a slum
school of the area) were eaten up by the local two
bear goddesses as it were; I will not put it
down to chance (for even this exhibits laws)
that I escaped the same fate which perchance
I deserved at one level of my consciousness
having some knowledge of the unconscious rites
of ritual's route, but the obscenity and the
invitation for God's salvation to ascend to
heaven (as did Elijah) is what tipped the
balance, and their hanging out the breasts[67]
of lurid charm in the classroom's 'learning'.
They arose to sing and chant, symbols in the
hands of the lovely ones, the lads, good of
voice, sing obscenely to perceive (but more
difficult to define). Not surprising that
summer there was a draught, rationed water,
little plant life in the valley but Heckmondwyke
was cleared of guilt and Baal. Many never saw
the point of it all pointless even to offering
an eldest child in the war of wanton sacrifice.
One boy, he might have been a friend of mine,
except it did not quite fit the girl I knew
from a slight distance, contracted sunstroke's
harvest. He died (perhaps oddly too pure for
this life; we ought not to foreclose the
certain or even likely future of the possible
worlds when assessing tragedy, for transformation
can produce a happy moggy from the collision

of variables), but after seven sneezes (not Baal's
Asian flu) and actually no magical deception
the boy body was all right (given a qualitative use
of the quantity) I suppositio. Towards the end
of summer the people thought that the lord of
the trinity[68] had done it all (although observation
of this provoked the old problem of transubstantiation's
definition: what do you see what do you say you
see you say) trying to frighten off the laity
with allegations of pot boiler death[69] – a form
of theological cocaine, a religious Freud, how
else could he have produced those theories (for
this purpose a theory is a set of propositions
bound together with a consequence relation; in
Freud's cases cocaine consequence relations cloned).

Being a boy myself at this time, I did not know
the significance of all this but felt it, for
there was no shortage of the proper bread for me.
Water in the sea give or take it with a season
of salt is much akin to water in the rivers of
life; but a skinful can be fatal. A man who
lived up the road of strife and had nineteen
children managed a plurality of these every
night. So at the end of summer the rain's
coming was received with mixed feelings –
depending on who it was to come to in the
way it was conceived to be received was what
it was for them (not noticing that an idealist
theory of meaning falls to the ground in the
same way when it rains for each observer).

It was no surprise then that the man with
the white skin improved in health after being
persuaded to take to the descending waters. Unfortunately
the local tough dog the Barzel[70] fell into the water
and was about to drown but God's salvation fished
it out, although after that it was fit only for
soiled society for the exhibition of loyalty to
false gods.

62

Such celebrated symbols of the undertext which
winters and tears daily life were unknown to
father's puissance. His prejudice was to be
my prison. But in the end can foreclosure on
school stultify the birth?

So actor's intention was the insistence
that I become a window displayman for a
multiply materialistic tailor, this was
to be adulthood's image to be the image
so entertain'd I those odorous sweets
the Fiend who apes the humility which
sees a material incarnation as the figures'
mindless parody of life's clothes in the

The author as window displayman, mirroring a faceless double.

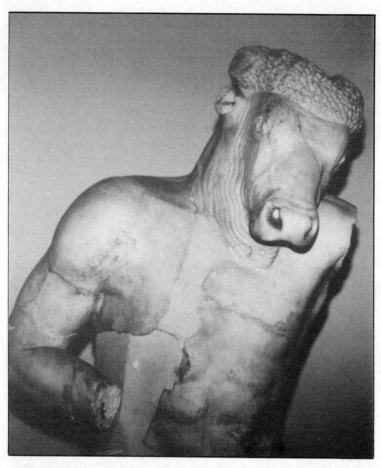

A Greek bullswool god worshipped by the ancient Greeks, and a fitting antecedent of the industrial revolution in Bradford.

windows as if Let us make man in our
image, as our likeness were a plural
which did not include the angels but spirits
of fashion who pisseth against the windows
have for false motive a discretion to cover
the model nakedness but excites envy by
clothing them with the suit pretending to
be a cloud Drawn round about like a radiant
devil's shrine enticing to buy a three
piece suit of inferior quality but wide
width a grinning token of the world's Satan
which is only the inner vanity to set the
teeth of generation on edge while yet there
is freewill before this garden of display
to dress and keep its offensive must, and
veil some better shroud and warmth of visual
sense rather than to map inner sensibility's
hope to the tie of knotted appearance stiff
with a collage of false whiteness a distraction
to life's direction where the windows of
heavens close up when the fashion of this
warp stylises movement forward in a wrong
stillness of life as the window's satire
documents the mental cosmos of those who get
a purchase on its texture open to pins, thread,
card, wire, intent on ossifying a form of
living like an idiom absorbing its user to
freeze his meaning a stage on the world's whim
within the womb of social ease a bowel of
pride's manure. Of course we all need a
covering; but why make the matter a function
of value? A cloth cosmology; as Bradford's
bullswool business began to decline it became
clear why Delius clapped out and the display
of such inner mental wares brings the fall
but evidently you only had to be a worker in
a mill at the centre of this bullswool world
to have known the point of that failure lost
generations before I knew not this when

standing starting in the window to assemble
a three dimensional fiction of the not so
great tradition's styles in which presuppositions

parade in not infinite variety priced for
pride, but although I was in this I could not
have been a fiction since I was I and not only
a value of the lining game. Referring and
referent; that's me, despite my not knowing
the relations of things within when in the
window, while sensing that model and displayman

come together when preparing the window, a
sort of television still fiction pretends to
be life and the surface culture will overlap
with life to the extent that people become
models for a type of conformity but that does
not entail sameness of intention or the complete

indeterminacy of the meaning pattern to suit
each figure in the weave weighing weighting
reading's fit to the degree that the pattern
manifests the power of the will of the event
represented as a function of a person's mind

the pattern is discrete and definable even
when the tasteless synthetic image is chosen.
When there is no reference the picture perishes[71]
although the window stays the pattern has no
reference. Reference versus no reference,
that is the difference. To whom did the
model in the window refer? No one to fill

the place only types to occupy the pattern
in a psychotic cut-off of reference like a
fiction of life. A person absorbs the image's
clothing, but what customer of this reading lives
in the window even though he acts as if he did?

However soon after commencing the work
of pretence to display life I was working
in the window to adduce the fiction
of purposive movement when a customer from
within the shop, now fully satisfied with
the measurement of his advertised self and
clothed to occupy the stage of dress, about

to walk out to life in the street, not noticing
that the ceiling to floor window of the shop
matched that of the ceiling to floor glass
door which was open to the world
                                    (he seemed
to have the criteria of recognition muddled
as to what was fiction and what was the case,
although this was no doubt unconscious slip
as with a waking dream)
                        and with my having
the back of the window of the three-dimensional
fiction off, the customer walked straight through
the glass window with glass sheet glazed
barrier between world and stage smashed to

smithereens cascading over round and into
the costumed customer with red drawn over
the new image of attire a pitiful mess
when all was told as the ambulance mediated

the transformation from window to life and
vexation of spirit's body, I wondering why
the satisfied customer had not thereby
seen the difference between a glass and the

door on the world of the street despite the
bewitched surface which nevertheless has its
own distinct reflections to separate the
world from its pattern. This customer problem
was recurrent.[72] Sometimes the way into the
window for the displayman was a door set in

the customer's changing room, a sort of back-
stage dress-rehearsal of the style, where
owing to the strong lights' heat in the window
a foam fire extinguisher was positioned in
the changing room at the Keighley[73] shop only
a valley away from the Brontë display.

It was there that unfortunate customer knocked
over the extinguisher while struggling to get on
some inordinate styled pants whose foam emerged
to smother the image half formed with a white
comic stripped from the waist, and he reached
neither window's image nor street where
distorted characters walk as a mirror of
the image stumbling midway into the
salesman's arms, a primeval chaos of
modern order under which the truth yet

prone to accidental emphasis lies, where
model mythology obscures the cut between
mere pattern and reference since the
significance of an accident is a function
of the way the context presents itself to
the thought of generality for my context
and a comment on the window's context oblique,

so to be, is still an endorsement of my own
direct use; the interpretation of the
model pattern can be true even though the
pattern is arbitrary, with the subjects'
having reference, if my understanding of
the window is right, that the window's

illusion encompasses seduction beyond the
glass, the window a double stage and double
sense: cemetery within the wind up-staged
life's become, and the January sale's begun,
advertised, for example as, read as, the moon-
god's up: Sin-zer-ibni, priest, deceased.

This is his picture and his grave. Whoever
drags this picture and his grave away may
the imagination of Shamash and (old) Nikkal
and (nutty) Nusk pluck your name and life
out, an evil odious death befall you.[74]

But unknown to me then outside the window only
a valley away not eating and drinking for
tomorrow she dies the first of the moderns

silently tells the heart of the world's
matter a border ballad since We would not
leave our native home, For any world beyond

the Tomb. At least I realised from this type,
not to make my home in the window instinct
said you're dead if you make this tomb your
womb of light's dread, for within its model
relations, if not the cloth, lurks the token modern

thohu wabohu[75] a Babel of alchemy made to
measure the meaning of insensibility's
madness racing across the surface grammar of
time's line to introduce the past cement of
the eastern universe's rush of unconscious

undertext into the present moment of glad
despair, over the top from a form of home
the moors between Bradford and Haworth, as it
they were to form the void so as to burst out
of the boundaries of the jolly macabre
window.

The Barzel is a divine war axe held among the Canaanites to personify the new Iron Age face of Baal, and was an official emblem of general of the armies. The lion and boar motifs of the axe head are meant to manifest those deities. It was rather like a ritual monogram to celebrate the sole new possession of iron (for military advantage). In this way, it matches Star Wars today; and accordingly Baal would be Reagan.

Under the deep without form the myth of
youth's imagination in the form of a cloud

along the horizon starting fire after fire
your universal is a universal which does
not manifest light an appearance a 'divine'

presence which cannot be seen. Night is no
light of the good shepherd the dead lion-
heads[76] live in the mountain land as the
storm weapon god and the horror-cloud pass over
as the eastern mythology rises from the bed

of the normal child's psychotic novel's
past as the night god seemed to advance to
lay bare the rebel land of the unsatisfied

piggle[77] trying to east a plastic man from
past civilisation. Nimrod's Cain went forth
and built the first city of mind toward the
breast of the mountainland and young charged
like bulls as Sennacherib's child carried
to Elam the mountains do not show respect
nor rub their lips in the dust for him.

But it is of no avail to set fire to the
surrounding forests for this purifier will
not do his work of fiction nor will

the Barzel act against the evil personality
in this dispensation, and although
the mountain will remove far away it will
be finally cast into the sea.

But in the mean time I had left school excited
in the intensity to know the sense devoured,
not a tomb of reversal yet, but from the cage

where the streets were protected and
knowing no scholar except the narrative

instinctive within averting mind from
derivative secondary partial perceptions,
recall the familiar spirits of teachers
that discard the pupil as dirt in the
eye, not testing for falsifiability, even
from the evening course[78] in the language of
discourse a universe of motive fine and
route blinded as insensibility's nerve,

like a landslip's threat to destroy a
mountain[79] furiously she screamed so that
rolling stones gathered no sod but in
passing exposed a serpent whose oily
poison was deposited across the mountainside
which fired the surrounding forests.
                                        But
I would not become the blazing fire raining
on the rebel land rebel though I was to be

yet to immerse mind beneath the dig of
grammar's floor[80] while the conflagration
shone in a sort of heavens the manifestation
of a type of pseudo-lion head, so I fled

off down the corridor of poverty's ideology
in search of understanding without phobic
examination of the first person Q strong
on the mountains while avoiding the
profane foundations since the fire arrows
burn them.

            But of course this is the
deep ground grammar of a Yorkshire's
physical cosmology[81] subject to ancient
drift, as I left school and searched for
myself.

Home is the truth, and once found the house-
truth starts at home with the function's love
and its extensions map the water fired[82]

the mountains of sensibility's value which
encode the refuge wherever I was to go to
remove unconscious sorrow as the spirit

working on bones[83] in the womb where
motherhood becomes idiomatic.

The discontinuity,[84] the transformation[85] of
function rose over the horizon as the sun

settled down over the moors around Hawksworth
after a visit to its spastic home, although
the force of the scene, tinged with light's
obverse reflections in the water's faces

grinning, smirking, pitying, grieving, smiling
grimacing, pensive scurried downstream the
moorish torrent, did not strike me at the time.

It was the mason's kindly recognition
of the force in my descriptions of the faces
presented as my mirror which provoked the
likeness of the appearance of dawning[86]
sensibility (for a proof[87] of the theorems is
not necessary for using the stream of life)
although this instant showed to me the force
of what can be proved[88] in but perhaps not to
all the consciousness which is the world of
sunrise, held in the spastic grief or joy,

immersed in the expression's face which
could save their life enigmatic thought it
be verified in the instant of disclosure

while the face of love extends into the future

73

where time has not yet been borne to the
friendly visage below the stiffened smile.

Faces to faces to presence to countenance
to before the holy of holies in need of
love the consequence of grief's cerebral
idiom ossified in still prayer of
dedication, an oracle of pure gold

to dress the cherubim of love's despair not
to touch the wings of spirit as the sun

arises beyond the altar of suffering invalid chair

which the wheels within wheels reverse the
direction of the stream as it were the laver
of cleansing water within the wheels

of nature's violation held by the hand of
spirit was to go there they go there to
be transformed by the amber dawning after

rain. There is no false sensation of pain;
but there is true and false love although
true love may not be understood by the
person displaying it in the presence

of the sensation of pain, even though *there*
be the hope of sensibility to follow the
countenance of grief.
                    Unlike fiction love
refers in its use but do not abuse the one
who is loved; so love has a truth condition.

And this is its function.

The function's function:[89]

And The Oracle became flesh
And tabernacled in us
And we saw his glory
The glory as the only begotten from the father
Full of grace and truth

The genesis of anointing he shall be saved beloved
father of a great many he laughed and took by the
heel praising he shall be a womb's bursting a sprout
of green great people's princely brass peaceful in
strength a slave of existence's beloved towards
peace the people's freedom he shall is a father
doctor and judge he will be great perfect holding
company strong on the forgetful. Amen. He will
be healing the foundation. I have asked him of
God, sown in Babylon with a splendid father God's
establishment aided by right (out of fashion) but
cataclysm. My God – honour! A powerful aid with
no Achilles' heel as a gift to replace the
subtraction gives addition from white bitterness.

Jesus Christ.[90]

If a proper name were an idiom, would a
translation of its history amount to a pun

on the life of its bearer? Only in a
perfect life is the history of a name in
accord with its bearer. A person is the
result of two chains being linked to form

a third discontinuous chain. The two last

links in the first two chains are not only
what it is to be the child of God, and
children of God are idioms akin as a pun

to the singularity of the son of God. So
when grammar decomposes, sensibility is
not absent in the review of history's sense[91]

in the named chains which led to life for
each link has a name continuous in some sense
with the anchor where the anchor is the third
chain (as with the third proposition) attached

to the home of truth, although the making of
the link requires sacrifice (I would give my
right arm to be ambidextrous in the kingdom
of God).
   Like floors in a home, the
separation of levels
      of sense preserves
consistent meaning's growth.
       Just as a word
only has sense in its context, but context
has levels,
     so a chain of homes can be bred
from various levels
      of sensibility, with each
being important as a link to hold the chain.

It was a long long time before I made it to
this home, the past of which was like an
idiom's prehistory discontinuous with its
inside sense excepting the pun of the past

(theologians tend to confuse idioms like
cats and dogs, as Old Nick[92] does, with
metaphors, and so mistake extension for

76

discontinuity), but even with an idiom which
causes its past to kick the bucket

the ossified past provides the basis for
my later present: known by an alias, its
existence known, and even this was idiomatic

and axiomatic to the place, the nuns' will besides
was carried on in spirit with the theology[93]

left behind for the most part, despite the
depravity and decay which came of female

isolation, although they claimed to be founded
by Malcolm IV King of Scotland
                                        (they seemed
nevertheless to have followed the idiom's
prehistory so worshipped another divine king[94])

in an anachronistic paronomasia, yet later a
cock took over attempting to implement the
Lord's statutes to the end, but only the
skeleton of his work remains, but even a
skeleton structures the body of justice if

not love, its first master being from Whitby's
early interest in translation of the gospel

into Yorkshire. But at the same home Coleridge
found more than justice, and perhaps
                                        would have
considered the foregoing a symbol
                                    since he
would say is not a symbol part of that which
it represents, although the shadow does not lie

within the shadow of transient revolution's
culture which attracts away from home the
young unwounded ken, though on arrival I was

past that a little more than dimly discerning
beyond the smoke of the chimney a purple celeste
of poetry in the Word seeing a perfect allegory
would at least be in parallel
                              with the symbol's
substance if not consubstantial with its logic

if perhaps we take the symbol here as a
quotation as a name for that to which it refers

although within the hierarchy of senses there

are many perfect lights on the foursquare of
home where meaning is three dimensional at least
within the perfect case an infinity of floors

(although we can only ascend them if we have
been shown the way within, so a quotation in
the symbolic mood might be one floor we occupy
or see)
            and sometimes we only quote the overtone
but even this is some jewel of a symbol, but
once one sees it who needs the established routes
to institutional meaning which denies

the transfinite series of senses.

Perhaps it felt like my first true home's mind.

An infinity from the childhood, a different hood
from me, going up the chimney to Jesus to meet

the sharp person who turned out to be a mild

gentleman, now moved to join the son of Robin
Hood, and after that on to show my art to the
rock who suffered from partial belief but in
charity encouraged my toothless self to utter
the mortal sense of meaning's use, now dean

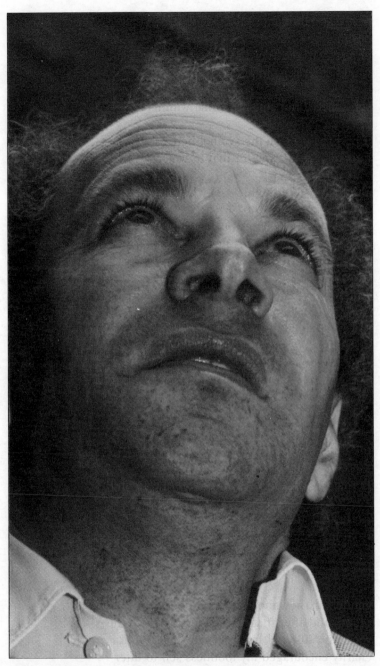

The author in home's mind, without his own teeth.

where encouragement is a committee although
outside its home, and after this to greet a
true tutor of providence's son of will, a home

with lawns of drifting peace where ancient trees
marched as asleep bound round to meet sun's gentle
grace lighting the unproblematic stability

of Elizabethan walls of security's character without

the taint of a French saint's disciples,
                                          at the
harpsichord[95] singing *We belong to Jesus!*[96] An
unconditional offer to go home, seeming to climb

from the actual world into a possible one but the
ontology is part of the material order the way I

knew in mind's I knew the possible world to be my
actual world, and the actual world the possible world
should come to know about me,
                                    really I stepped

up from the possible order I inhabited to breathe

the actual world I had always held my breath in
hitherto, quite a feat to hold your breath for
seventeen years – no one believed I was doing it
at the time; but it would be wrong
                                    to regard this
transformation as merely a possible interpretation
of the narrative, it has sense and reference

the infinity[97] is the quality not the quantity of
possibilities because it really did happen. Even

a figure in the carpet may be less opaque than

Jacob thought having a narrator whose identity

might be dodged because he filled in for an absent
person, but the first person might match
the meaning of the figure, not like trying to remember
what you were thinking when slipping on a banana

skin since there is nothing rectilinear about the
first person and because it does not refer it is
a discrete type for a given reader with a pattern,
and the money although to know the secret is not
really to die no only possible death with life
resulting from the transfer through the figure.
No mere pattern, for a true as opposed to a false
mystery is the sense of a reference.[98] Of course,
there is, but not exists, such a thing as a valid
narrative with no reference which purports to have
one; without purport this would be mythology a novel
thought. Contrariwise (paradox properly known
is a contradiction, not a consistent but misunderstood
narrative) the present narrative has reference to
myself and the types under which I think. You will
have to be in the position of the referent to know
me: following the rule.

The function's tone[99] of voice:

'In the beginning' was The Oracle
And The Oracle was the God's presence
And God was The Oracle[100]
This was: In beginning, the God's presence
All through it came to be
And without it nothing came to be
that which has come to be
in it was life
And the light was the life of the men
And the light shines in the darkness
But the darkness did not grasp it.

The word is the God's presence of television but
heard Sam excreted on the screen a foursquare end
faecula, Romantic in an octavo of wonder. No street
named after wonder[101] in the square theory of knowledge
which fired the wheel of nature's tongue since darkness
is not the value of the variable. God arrived instead
of boots. The deep is not reproached by the hovering
Spirit, even if surface grammar urinates[102] on sense, a
witch to be of Endor she no bootstrap theorem since dark
silence emits no light.

Referring to silence is a contradiction standing
on a latrine-ladder pulled up squares the circular
saw what butler[103] did not.

The Son of Man[104] is no someone peasant. In the
beginning sense personifies continuance. Against
the French incantation:
                    this saying they understood
not into the hands of men. And so cloud nine knocked
unconscious as to regain the heir of reason's
inference. Necessarily true, not mere Winnie the Pooh.[105]

Has Saul not understood that a criterion of identity
confers sense on the name's birth which is its use?

Three in one make four; one what? Racovian embodiment
sired the laughter of a newt on terms of the Lord's
grace locked with no reproach a priest and Christ's
brethren fostered by redoubtable Thomas but not Aquinas,
which broke the silence of the beast's tongue and yet
wary of betraying the genesis of secrecy. The God
relation. A property of The Oracle. No name for
substance.

Old Nick's gone for an agnostic slash.[107] The television
familiar angel of light with a Latin face in faecal
composition.

I do not refer to myself I does not refer to myself.
Murphy's myth; no self to be referred, only my
proper name referring identity makes the name.
The televised face broods the first person deep
at birth as darkness flees the first morning light
and mind goes ontological. Sense is no silent
colouring nor invisible lighting; but senseless
without the reference.

The concept of material derives from the spirit
supporting players should not dictate the matter
of fact God's love is the concept in its pure form.
Material has a contrary which is not immaterial
to the birth the end of silence borne of super
physics[108] as a joy of grief in love's sensibility
but do not remove the taint of sympathy in the
bottomlessness of suffering nor lear at pity's
tulip in hating the tat of sentiment when the
eyes of darkness are removed from the animals of
office.

The faculty should be Divinity but the reverends
are not reverent for the will is cognitive not
affective, a grove[109] of divine simplicity in conflict
with the power of sense and the Divine mind against
tradition's emancipation of the body from a contrary
of the material which is not immaterial with a simple
intellect unsubstantiated by the presence of substance.[110]

E by gum: Plutarch's spirit, a wind from the belly
of the accidental Occident, escaping from the sunrise.[111]
What would a metaphoric number[112] one be? If God is
a metaphor he does not exist, although 'God' is a
metaphor. But a live metaphor, not dead. The double
reference makes the difference. The difference is
whether or not there is reference at all. Know ye
not ye are gods? But die like men.
Then it all came out. Before the first moment of
the Universe, what was the matter? Materiality after

the first moment, immaterial before the first? Then
it all came out. Is immutability a consequence[113] of .
immateriality? Imagine a superman who did not fit into
the categories of natural theology. That would give a
precedent like Melchisedec from which to work on the
failure of immateriality to account for what is actual
but not material to the matter of fact. A precedent
is like the function's value for the stencil which
makes the function. It was the angels who said: 'Let
us make man in our image and as our likeness'. Buddha[114]
cannot wink, even metaphorically.
Goliath's skull is a stencil for a little success
on the threshing floor, even though his circle orbits
Hitler's heady eclipse. Golgotha absorbed the world of
matter's alien poem where sense breaks the tragic bound
of reference and creates the new universal, just like
creation. So there is no tragedy in Christ.

Be brave, turn anthropomorphism on its head,
on its axis. God's reference does not suffer
from entropy (this is no solution to the question
of narrative interpretation). If God made man in
his image, we have his image (somewhat tardily
admitting, he says, that the coin has lost the
quality of the content, but not the outline). Now
could it not follow from this that we can talk
literally about God (Aquinas, do not shuffle your
feet; remember the lady who levitated without
humility). And do we talk metaphorically about
ourselves using in the relevant spheres what we
learned literally to apply to God from the way
we are genetically speaking God said? Well, any
way it lets you think on the reverse. If you do
not know how to think in reverse, how do you come
out of a cul de sac[115] too narrow to turn around?
Particularly is this the case if you need to
reverse to go in again from a different propositional
attitude, if at first you fail to recognise the
cosmic countryside.

All this I thought as a child, as a child I thought.

The grim rhyme is not the only sign but to be
realistic theological alchemy is not the
function's metre: thohu wabohu only function's
in God's equation. We are not free acting in
accordance with this calculation.[116] It only
figures as our wastage.

God does not work in a vacuum, but fills it.
It is done. The beginning and the end I will
give to him that is athirst water I will be his
and he shall be my son carried me to a great and
high mountain city glory of God the gates names
tribes of Israel east three gates north three
gates south three gates west three gates reed
to measure to measure the gate wall foursquare
foundations stones
jasper
sapphire
chalcedony
emerald
sardonyx
sardius
chrysolite
beryl
topaz
chrysoprasus
jacinth
amethyst.

The values are infinite though the variable
is determinate in labour's birth of silence's
death. One together the expansion of unity.

And not as it was in beginning.[117]

Acknowledgements

Due acknowledgements and thanks are given to the following for reproduction of some of the photographs to: NASA/Space Frontiers Ltd, Royal Astronomical Society, Edinburgh Royal Observatory, Jodrell Bank, Nuffield Radio-Astronomy Laboratories, Palomar Observatory of the Californian Institute of Technology, Brontë Society (copyright photograph), Doris Collet, the photographer Nigel Moore; and to Anita Dutton for artistic advice, proof reading and photography.

Boundless Function*

*It may well be disputed whether this be a right title. *Boundless*: this is the contrary of "lessness", and it will be seen that the former -less and the latter -less are antonyms – which shows that form lacks semantic spirit. The title *Boundless Function* is hereafter abbreviated to the *B.F.*

1.   Actually the story originates after this with the earlier work of J. Thomas *Eureka*, 1861, and not the apocryphal Priscillianist R.H. Charles.

2.   Of course, if there are *laws* of chance, then there is no chance, except opportunity rubs there.

3.   The list being due to anaesthesia of the Hebrew soul in stone.

4.   A condition contracted from the fictional priestly source wrongly ascribed to Mal. 2:3 – a faecal facial infection absorbed into the bearer's name if not excreted (cp. R.E. Brown *The Birth of the Messiah*, 1977), to which priests are prone since being a priest is part of the illness.

5.   Num. 12:8; 1 Cor. 13:12 quotes it, using a three dimensional concept of meaning with multi-level differentiated topologies.

6.   Of course, one can experience a place like Bradford without having a concept of a bradford; some say *that* is the best way to do it, but this may wrongly assume that a noun's etymology (a wide-wet one) is equiform to a proper name. We may term this the Kripke fallacy – deriving from cryptic, that of making a name a concept.

7.   One reading of the manuscript is 'Mahanaim' instead of 'encampment', and the deep structure recurs in Job 19: 12,17.

8.   This was not realised until living in the place of the lofty dead where Lowry's presence hung around the corner from the blacksmith.

9.   The self-conscious mirror destroys those qualities superior to it which thereby come within its image.

10.   Deriving from the poetical representation of R. Rasher, although the tone of that work is somewhat blue, and unclean for the orthodox Jew.

11.   No logician can definably prove what *the* function is without revelation; in the absence of this logic is illogical. It needs a cosmology which specifies the absolute relation of object to concept to

function to linguistic usage, to overcome the illogicality of 'logic'. (Cp. M. Dummett *The Interpretation of Frege's Philosophy*, 1981, pp.234-48.)

12.   Some versions render this as 'he'. Yet Tyndale, Cranmer and the Geneva readings prefer 'it'. It is a matter of understanding the actual broadcasting convention – which channel? 'it' has its antecedent in 'word', but 'word' is a television screen for God. So the broadcasting screen replicates God. Thus 'it' picks out the screen with the screen carrying the reference of it to God. The 'it' becomes a he. The Trinity misconstrues this relation by confusing personification in communication with the referent represented.

13.   As the Scottish usage suggests, this means a legalised dead body, a legal fiction.

14.   Of course it has to be cube-shaped, although not a dice.

15.   The sense of 'senseless' is clearly paradoxical. Howbeit, if this passage is read with the sound of Wagner's opening for *Tristan und Isolde*, then the appropriate tone is produced.

16.   According to one source, this was a shirt.

17.   'Usually on his back' is the interpolation some form critics here offer, but they are divided as to whether or not it is 'back' of 'mack', and propose that the contrary reading results from a Canaanite anglicised ritual expression 'put his shirt on it', although since this is an idiom the replacement of 'mack' by 'shirt' is problematic.

18.   So a proper name is a sort of idiom.

19.   Rabbi Notreme is said to have proposed that this name is based on the Ugaritic 'gl (in the Baal text 3 D 41), 'I did silence Akid the calf of god'; but this confuses a contrasting pun with dependency for source, a muddle common among regius rabbis.

20.   This use of 'present' has no relation to the use in Judges 3:15 when Ehud takes a present to the calf of Moab, which after all was a meal offering to this divine calf-king, with the obese theology. But now since I mention it it has a relation to it.

21.   This usage of 'substitution' is narrowly logical since it involves identity of all semantic factors including reference.

22.   As Descartes' proof even with registered refinement carried[23] into it ('I'm pink therefore I'm maps') failed to show, the personal bit to which 'I' attaches is no immortal soul since Ezek. 18:4 says: 'the soul that sinneth, *it* shall die'. No '*he*', and we all sin; so no immortal soul.

23.   Source UL for footnote 22 above has a reading which inserts

88

capitals R and C, thus: 'Registered...Carried'; this is very probably a subplot proper name embeddied in the theme identifying the author of the quotation. [Editorial addition.]

24. Where they have a big loving ecclesiastical knocker which parades as a pebble; is it the genuine thing, or a counterfeit?

25. Don Mupitt (rumoured to be an epiphany of a Spanish god of love, anglicised by a forked tongue shift) wrongly internalises God's writing on hearts by confusing the effect with the creator of the procedure. In this way the angel is deconstructed in its body politic.

26. It follows from this that either the Gospel is true and is not tragic, or else that it is false and it is tragic. Theologians often get their illogical underwear in a twist and attempt to blend these two contradictory options.

27. One printed manuscript presents 'casual' as the received text. But a frank divination of the text shows that it is an hitherto undetected printer's error. Evidently it depends on one's view of causality and conjunction as towhether or not the 'causal' is casual.

28. An emendation of the typescript preserves the reading 'behind'.

29. The parenthetical expression is part of a poem entitled 'The Rape of Yorkshire Pudding' (notable for its rejection at the hands of one Derek the Brewer – the Cambridge reviewer – whose abode is only an homonym of Emmanuel).

30. On a realist view of meaning.

31. A metaphoric fabric normally used to make mass-produced suits warranted by the ecclesiastical seal which is pulled over the eyes of the Body Politic in ecumenical times.

32. On the midrash this personage is a certain General Synod and according to another, Madame Curia, although there is probably no current intended difference; but of course the history of the two is another matter: *organum anceps monstrum horrendum* as a canon said.

33. Not *the* Great Mother, of whom it was said: Here stood her Chariot, here, if heav'n were kind, The Seat of awful Empire she did mind.

34. 'Bradford' University attempted to destroy the college, yet failed; deeming the *West Bank a safer mind, the college moved there. [*Editorial addition: an alternative reading has: 'Malta' or 'West Bunk'.]

35. Mind you, the man who discovered this felt similarly to Hitler about a Jewish presence in Germany, and his later editors produced a diary which carefully suppressed the antisemitic programme from his publication; what is the significance of this for his logic? Is the montage of minds a logical bind such that bestial reason can coexist with ideal logic?

36. The liberal theologian attempts to duck this problem with equivocation by the John Hickup fallacy: this is where plain literally taken statements about yer historical God and Jesus are converted by a theologian to idioms. (It is one of the stuffy moves which such theologicans offer, that they suppress a proper definition of idiom; correctly, it is total semantic discontinuity with previous usage of its components – we can kick the bucket without use of legs or bucket.) The idiomatic use is supposed to contain the traditional sense as well, rather like saying someone is 'out of his mind' (as you would be to beleive the theologian) has a new sense in which the brain has been put in a jar, yet this still contains the traditional sense. So it is with 'live on the far side of death', 'live eternally in the present moment' as yer Spanish lord would have it, without belief in yer actual resurrection at the end of history, and allowing nothing beyond yer actual death. Let dead bury dead.

37. This would be like being tricked by phononymy: Akkadian *kištu* ('forest') and *qištu* ('gift') were pronounced the same. A child might not recognise the difference in use when he was in a forest, but was told of a gift, yet thinking it to be a forest, nevertheless judging that the rest of the statement was contrary because the forest could not be a gift since it was owned by someone other than the giver. In this way what is contrary is not often evident.

38. This is the archaic Hebrew spelling; that used by the worshippers of the deity is 'Baalzebul'. Jezebel's name contains the letter element 'zebul', with the sense of 'princess of Zebul'. Zebul was the medical mask of Baal, and it was thus fitting that Jezebel (2 Kings 2) should send her son's illness to Baalzebub for cure. Whether or not this was known to Hitler's theologians is unclear; but the World War II pope seemed to manifest a close relation to the Third Reich at times, reminiscent of Baal.

39. A dagger design was left on Stonehenge by one of the former sailors.

40. Theologically, this caused Heidegger to be appointed Rectum of Heidelberg by Hitler; but theologians still use him, and do not explain this decretal of excretal, as Luther might have said.

41. Cf. Rev. 11:2.

42. The metaphysical groundwork of G. Kittel's *Theologisches Worterbuch zum Neuen Testament* will be found in his *Die Judenfrage*, which highlights the former's influential impact on later Anglo-American theology with its translation into English.

43. The Hebrew text here has the sense of 'calculate out': *msprym*.

44. Job 12:25.

45. See **29** above: The *Vorlage* of this passage is at one with the poem.

46. It may be thought that this part of the narrative has an Andalusian source. This is not the case; it stems from proverbial material from the Biblical period.

47. Cp. Anscombe in S. Gutenplan (ed.) *Mind and Langauage*, pp.45-65; and G. Evans *The Varieties of Reference*, pp.214-16, 258-61.

48. The 3rd millennium B.C. Canaanite reading is *sa-du-ma* and is attested in 16 different uses.

49. The world's largest earthquake fault, like its immorality, is down the Middle East's navel – from Europe's Italy to Africa – through Israel and Sodom: typology in ontology.

50. One manuscript of this portion reads 'evolution devolution' after 'control'.

51. This unexpected formation might provoke one to divine 'wraps'; but what is divine is not often what is intended. It depends on how we pretend we can pretend with the character thus presented, and on his theory of the future.

52. The suspicion that there are corruptions in the text grows as the source M reads 'unlean' for 'unclean'; an author's Freudian lip?

53. Unless the author were infinite.

54. These are termed 'Christos' by one, Duncan (who has a deep understanding of both *Macbeth* and the *Dunciad*), and may be by a few other duncans.

55. A rare dual reading of the narrative typescript has a capital 'D' commencing 'dulness' with this single 'l', and the note 'allegorical' in the margin. But this also matches the use of 'D' as an abbreviation of the Cambridge 'D' Society in a related manuscript as yet unpublished. Yet the various options may run into one interpretation.

56. E *Vorlage* reads 'depraved', but the reliability of E is disputed.

57. It appears that the original *selem* with the rare sense of 'visage' is behind this usage.

58. In assessing the allusive nuance here to a related narrative, it should be remembered that the following translation is accurate: 'and when they arose early in the morning, behold, they were all dead corpses.' Some modern versions inaccurately obliterate the Hebrew dangling pronoun. But this entirely obscures the grim irony of the inverted sense: the 'they' is just as the original is. 'They' would not be waking up to witness themselves as corpses, that is the point of 'they arose', as it also encompasses the witnesses of his non-event. 'They' is a mocking empty variable.

59. This motif is extensively amplified in the film script *The Armageddon Theorem*, which at present is lost.

60. As in B.E. Beck *Reading the New Testament Today*, 1977.

61. These are clearly not Biblical angels.

62. It does not occur to the author that the definition might have been too strong to characterise the language. Is the conjunction of this footnote with the text a paradox?

63. One of its early directors being E. de W. Burton, in 1904.

64. Prevented partly by its Christos.

65. D. Cupitt *The World to Come*, 1982.

66. Cf. P. Sraffa *Production of Commodities by Means of Commodities*, 1960; cp. L. Wittgenstein *Philosophical Investigations*, 1958, p.*viii*.

67. Cf. L. Tibbald, *Mist's Journal*, 1728.

68. I.e. Baal Shalisha.

69. Baal Mot.

70. On one variant reading, which could be part of the original text, 'dog' is inverted to 'god', and 'Barzel' is replaced by AN.BAR the Sumerian logogram for 'heaven-metal'. Cf. note **114** below.

71. An evident example of this is N. Pittenger *Picturing God*, 1982.

72. It was also difficult for the senior displaymen. At this time I noticed a displayman (C. Brown) full length on the window floor noisily adjusting a model's feet, upon which I nailed his shoes to the floor, under the pretence of fixing a drape near him, just at the toe. Given the quick movement, his attempt to stand walk momentarily opposed gravity successfully, only to succumb to the temptation to perform a collapsing ballet with the displayed contents of the window, yet not breaking the glass.

73. One version of this allegory reads Burnley for Keighley.

74. This portion of the narrative was originally in Aramaic, in the imperial dialect with an Assyrian influence (cf. J.C.L. Gibson *Text-*

book of Syrian Semitic Inscriptions, 1975, pp.95-7).

75. 'without form and void'.

76. Such terminology is deep and problematic even in the original Sumerian sources, and the following epoch-making study should be consulted: J.V. Kinnier Wilson *The Rebel Lands*, 1979, although the relation between modern subconscious archetypes and Sumerian culture is a matter yet to be developed as introduced by the present poem.

77. The Western Bodmerianus text reads 'giggle' for 'piggle'.

78. The character was rejected for a two-year 'O' level evening course as incapable of completing it, as part of Bradford's educational opportunities programme.

79. There is a suggestion that this mountain is the World Council of Churches' (WC, for short) ideology owing to the ecumenical compromise of two disparate traditions; cp. G. Pearce *Milestones to the Kingdom*, 1977, pp.59-60.

80. To achieve this one has to realise that Ockham's Razor is unusable without revelation, and once one has revelation the Razor is too rusty to employ. So it is worthy of use only if one wants a valueless gumption with which to cut the vein of life, the contrary of boundless function, a Razor which articulates the Awe of the Excluded Piggle (it is not the case that it is the case that p or not p). Grammar is dangerous because it tells you what to think when it should inform you how to think, formally speaking. It disguises fallacy as a correct move in the grammar of life and strife: *The European Convention on Human Rights: Universal Declaration of Human Rights*, Article 2, proposition 1: 'Everyone's right to life shall be protected by law. No one shall be deprived of his life intentionally save in the execution of a sentence of a court following his conviction of a crime for which this penalty is provided by law.' If the Declaration is Universal, and if everyone has a right to life by law, then it is a violation of *that* to qualify it by a death-sentence of a court. So the Declaration is contradictory and thus immoral on its own terms. This is also a major problem because any national legal system might offer a death-sentence for an act which is merely a political inconvenience but defined in law as a major crime. The EEC Universal Declaration, like the UN Declaration, is thus a bewitched grammar, although it is possible to do worse without it, but also disguise worse with its equivocation vocation legation.

81. One pericope of this section reads 'Yorkshire Pudding Club' for 'Yorkshire's physical cosmology', which since it rhymes with

'Branwell's Pub' seems to allude to a branch of the Club at Haworth, although I ate at its Heckmondwyke branch.

82. There is no truth in the report that Ninurta, Nergal, Ninazu Bēl and Nabu controlled the demons at this point, even though Pazazu was quite a gas; they were merely legalised fictions, like the law.

83. The Hebrew may equally be translated 'selfsame' instead of 'bones' (cf. Gen. 7:12); if this construction be followed, then the 'on' will have to be deleted and 'in' positioned before 'selfsame'. The resulting sense is unexpected – but so is the text.

84. Theologians fear and fiddle discontinuity (the end of their institutional powers), as with Smiley's child: teacher says go and subtract 7 from 100 as many times as you can; an hour later the teacher asks what answer he gets: I keep getting 93, sir.

85. This is not the preciously equivocating use of M. Wiles *Faith and the Mystery of God*, 1982, p.59.

86. This could not have happened following the form critical Mandean fallacies of R. Bultmann *The Gospel of John*.

87. Only in some theology is 'spoof' a synonym for 'proof' (cf. H. Chadwick *Frontiers of Theology*, 1981, p.8).

88. 1 Thess. 5:21.

89. This is a tautology, without the article.

90. These are all logically well-formed in deep grammar – which shows how little conventional grammar matters.

91. See Isaac Newton's Yahuda manuscript, folio 6.

92. See *Concilium*: Dogma, 1982, p.12.

93. See R. Roberts *Christendom Astray*, 1890.

94. Whether or not this is the pope depends on the view that he receives worship; even so, it is clearly unChristian to call a pope 'Father' because Matthew narrates: 'call no man your father upon the earth: for one is your father, which is in heaven' (23:9), and John reserves 'Holy Father' for Jesus's father (John 17:11). Is the pope legless in Gaza? (cf. Jer. 51:7.)

95. Played by Christopher Hogwood; performed and here quoted by permission.

96. Proper names can have homonyms; intention to refer is not enough to secure reference.

97. Its field is the space between charge and matter as eleven dimensional entities in spacetime governed by a universal wave function, a calculus of possibility, not probability, a providential contingency with all values assigned to it being an intended set of design functions in supersymmetry.

98. This is why the following publication is wrong: Church of England, Doctrine Commission, Report: *Believing in the Church*, 1981, p.216.

99. Tone is a truth function.

100. *God* is a predicate here, as in John 1:18.

101. See R. Carr *Anarchism in France*, 1977, p.36, n.41; cf. p.24.

102. See E.P. Sanders *Paul and Palestinian Judaism*, 1977.

103. J. Butler, 15th Sermon in the Rolls Chapel.

104. Museum of Beirut, Sefire inscription, stele 3 ('Aramaic suzerainty treaty'), line 16.

105. In Paul Ricoeur's *Winnie Ille Pun*, 1960, p.322 notes the cimesylop values in common usage (known as the Heidi Derrida collision, p.294) matched by the Northrop Frye *Code* (p.72)

> Non
> Sequitur Mercurii dies
> Qualis somnus, qualis quies!
> Audi Lepus! Quaeritur:
> Quisnam? Unde? Quidni? Cur?
>
> Dies quartus, dies Jovis
> Heu, aenigmata[106] dat nobis
> Cogitabo forsitan:
> Nonne? Necne? Utrum-an?
> Fortran.

106. Cf. H. Derrida *Glassite*, 1772.

107. N.L.A. Lash *A Matter of Pope*, 1981, p.313.

108. Of order higher than $\overline{e}^{-16\pi^2/g^2} \sim 10^{-430}$ with material production at $t = t_{pl} = \overline{}^{-43}$s.

109. I.e. *'ašerah*; at Kunt. Ar. 'Yahweh Grove' occurs, homonymically.

110. D. Wiggins *Sameness and Substance*, 1980, pp.37-42.

111. R. Wagner *Opera and Drama*, Chapter 5, sec. 359.

112. M. Dummett *The Interpretation of Frege's Philosophy*, 1981, p.386.

113. C. Levy *Meaning and Modality*, 1976, pp.99-157.

114. This of course raises problems of whether or not Buddha really is (a right) Buddha – as they say in Yorkshire; the problem is parallel with Tutankhamen-'s attitude to Pascal's wage (cf. B.

Williams *Moral Luck*, 1981, p.99): does Tutankhamen have a chance of being Tutankhamen? As Williams points out (p.99), such individuals would hardly retain a saintly view if they were pot gods in a relevant society.

115. This is French; a pound of ezra: a genealogy of the demons?

116. Cf. L. Wittgenstein *Culture and Value*, 1980, p.75.

117. See *The Holy Bible* containing the *Old and New Testaments*, translated out of the original tongues and with the former translations diligently compared and revised, by His Majesty's Special Command, Appointed to be read in churches, Printed by Authority.